W9-CJI-879

A *Complete* *Guide to* Effective Excuses

by **Wayne Allred**

Illustrated by David Mecham

✦ A WILLOW TREE BOOK ✦

Published by:
Willow Tree Book
Box 516
Kamas, Utah
84036

Copyright 1996 by E. Wayne Allred.
All rights reserved. No part of this book may be
reproduced or transmitted in any form or by any means
(electronic or mechanical, including photocopy, recording,
or any information retrieval system) without the written
permission of the author.

ISBN 1-885027-05-2

First Edition published in 1993.
Second Edition with additions published in 1996.

Design by David Mecham
Printed in the United States of America

This book is dedicated to
all those poor folks who have
passed from this Earthly existence
whose lives might have been preserved
by any one of the excuses, explanations,
or groveling techniques contained
herein.

Contents

You may have noticed that there is no introduction in this book. Of course I have a very good excuse for this and no, the dog didn't eat it. At least, not the version that I was typing because what happened was that when I sat down to write it, I was drinking an Italian soda and while waiting for the computer to boot up, I took a drink. Just at the exact moment when I was raising the glass to my lips, I got a sudden urge to cough. While fighting that urge for a split second, I inhaled and snorked a bunch of Italian soda up the wrong pipe. It wound up in my nose which made me sneeze at the same time I was spilling the rest of the soda all over my keyboard.

After this, not only was typing very slow since it takes considerably more time to lift fingers off from sticky keyboards than non-sticky ones, but in my effort to hurry, while using all of the strength in my fingers, I lost my balance. This caused me to fall off from my chair and while falling to the floor, my head must have hit the corner of the table which also could explain why I have such large bags under my eyes, a tendency to misuse big words and insomnia. In any case, I was unconscious until it was too late for me to submit the introduction to the publisher. And so, thinking that I must have gone off to Canada on vacation having forgotten to write the introduction, my editor inserted some lame biographical information in its place, which I replaced with this.

Thank you.

Assignment:

7,000 page report
on topic of your choice.

or

A GOOD EXCUSE

1

How I Became an Expert on the Subject of Excuses

I am sure that I speak for most higher life forms; business managers, teachers, parole officers, spouses, aliens, pets, and creditors, when I say that there are few things in this world that give greater enjoyment than listening to a good excuse. One must ask what kind of person, who even considers himself a part of the human race, doesn't feel the tingle of anticipation as they hear someone begin to describe how their pet wombat ate their homework? What kind of a slime ball wouldn't get a tear in his eye hearing one of his employees explaining that the reason why he didn't get that urgent report completed today was because his brother-in-law's great aunt, once removed, had died of an exploding varicose vein? A person would have to be an

3

insensitive jerk not to have her heart swell with emotion while she listens to some loser blubber through a yarn about not wanting to pass on genetic tendencies toward incontinence and weak arches as an excuse for not making a commitment to marriage. That's right, it's a primal part of our human nature to want to be lifted to the heights of expectations and pulled to the very depths of emotional misery, to be a part of this monumental human drama we call excuse making.

That's why it disturbs me so much when someone comes to me late, or un-prepared, and I find myself getting all excited to hear this great explanation...and then the person proves to be totally inept at making excuses, he or she can't lie his or her way out of a wet paper bag.

Not long ago, while teaching a high school English class, I got to the point that I was so disillusioned that I was about to leave the profession out of disgust. It should have been a great year too because I had a few "special" students who would never come into my class without being either totally unprepared or late. On a good day they would be both. They kept raising my expectations day after day after day, but when it came time for them to deliver, I would be forced to endure lame excuse after lame excuse. Whenever I really thought about it, I became terrified at the thought of these and other even more inept students going out into the world so unprepared that after getting beat up regularly for being such saps, they would eventually die of starvation or become registered Democrats.

Now, don't get me wrong, many of these students had a good deal of natural ability; some, who made bad excuses, could speak their lines like vacuum salesmen, but they desperately needed a creative excuse; some had the ability to think up some doozies, but just couldn't present them convincingly; and then there were others who could fake sincerity like young politicians, but who had both dorky excuses and bad deliveries. Rare was the student who could put it all together and deliver an excuse that would really get the job done.

As a teacher, my natural inclination was to send them to the library to do a research paper on the problem. But I didn't have to do that very many times before I began to say to myself, "Hey, there isn't any authoritative material written about excuses and their application." I concluded that the only responsible thing to do was write a book on the subject which would help the thousands of students, the dozens of workers, and the billions of common, ordinary people, who don't have a deep enough understanding of excuses to have a realistic chance of succeeding in today's kind and gentle world...and which would vault me to the pinnacle of success as the world's premier authority on the subject. So, thanks to the encouragement of my students, my wife, my analyst, and the I.R.S. agent assigned to my case, and as a way of becoming powerful, rich and famous, I have written this book.

Actually, I would have written it much earlier except I had a sprained index finger from improperly catching a cast-iron Frisbee at the park last summer, and also I didn't have enough time because my wife made me clean up the mess I made while she was gone, when the septic tank backed up all through our living room because I flushed a dead hamster down the toilet while she was gone for two weeks and it dried up, which made it harder to clean (I really had intended to clean it earlier), and because I'm not feeling totally myself lately because I have nodules on my spleen, unusually bad gas, and fallen arches, and I don't sleep well at night because some large rodent runs around in the ceiling from 12:00 to 2:15 every night.

I am about to make a very bold statement.

A very bold statement.

Nothing about your life is as important as your skill with excuses. Let me phrase that another way. You are what you explain away. This is undeniably true. Some of the most miserable, revolting, chiseling, scummy, and disgusting people you will ever know, owe their wretchedness, ugliness, ignorance, poverty, and bad personal hygiene to poor excuse skills. Some of the most successful, good-looking, sophisticated, popular, respected, rich, and intelligent people in the world today will tell you that they owe their entire success to some critical moment when their highly-trained mouth spontaneously spewed forth a brilliantly conceived, correctly structured, and competently delivered excuse. Take as an example, my friend Craig, who received a call from a potential employer with a job offer to operate the street sweeper in a small town in North Dakota. He delivered a properly executed excuse to decline and the following day received a call from the revolutionary council in the South Pacific island country of Guano, who wanted him to come and assume his rightful position as sovereign for life and patriarch of his harem of 92 wives. Now, you can't just sit back there and say, "sure, but who's going to call and offer me a harem and a kingdom?", because everyone's situation is different, and because I have statistics. And I could show them to you if I could remember where they are. And I think these particular statistics, if I remember what the guy told me about them, would show that some day, statistically speaking, even you will definitely need good excuses for any number of very good reasons.

Very Good Reasons

Good reason #1: You will need excuses in order to keep from losing your job. Every day of your working life you screw up, and one of these days you're going to get caught. If you haven't mastered the skills taught in this book, I will have no sympathy for you when you find yourself driving a street sweeper in North Dakota. Now I know that some of you are sitting there and smugly saying something like; "They can't fire me, I have tenure. I'm not required to care what my superiors or anyone else thinks," Wrong! In this day of tight budgets, down-sizing, and outcome oriented strategies, even if they can't fire you, you will need good excuses to keep from having to do things that you don't want to. At some point, you may even need to justify keeping your job description, to keep from having your job title changed to something unimportant sounding like "clerk," or "salesman."

Good reason #2: Some people need good excuses to keep from having to spend an entire evening with people who are as interesting as a presidential speech or a good math problem, or from being forced to do something like listen to accordion music in stereo while watching a neighbor's home movies, or even worse, from getting stuck with a blind date arranged by Cousin Bart with a guy who is a known child molester, who wears polyester bell-bottom pants and gold chains, and whose breath smells like Kibbles and Bits.

Good reason #3: Some need good excuses in order to give their spouse a way out. There are

8

millions of spouses who desperately want to believe their wife or husband's excuses, so they don't have to file for divorce. Like my cousin Bernice, who is married to George, whom she doesn't especially like, but who has a nice house and lots of money, and if they got in a messy divorce he would find out that she has a boyfriend, Bob, who everyone else knows about and who he suspects, but he doesn't really want to know because he has a girlfriend, Alice, who he takes care of financially, and both of their kids would sue them for child's divorce for making them eat brussel sprouts and because they only have one Nintendo. And so you see, that in their case, a well-conceived excuse just saves a lot of people much needless pain, heartache and expense.

Good reason #4: Some people need good excuses to avoid placing people in awkward social situations, like when you don't know what to say because just at the moment when you know that your house is so filthy and smells so foul that an olfactory disadvantaged cape buffalo would get the dry heaves, some socially important person who you need to impress, drops by unexpectedly to ask you to host the Governors tea this afternoon because she heard that your house is big enough to seat 88 third-world dignitaries and their concubines. I'm sure that now you can clearly see how important it is to be a good excuse maker.

Be An Expert: In order to be an effective

excuse maker, however, you must take it seriously. It's not something that you can just be casual about. A person must be a student of the true art and they must be continually thinking in terms of excuses if they want to avoid getting flabby. (Incidentally, there is nothing worse than a flabby excuse, except maybe getting your lips caught in a table saw blade, or having your appendix removed by a sado-masochistic nurses aid with a wood-burning set and a fork.)

Now, we admit that some of the excuses in this book could be characterized as "intellectual excuses." They are on a very high creative plain. We know from experience that some people are nervous about using excuses that are very creative. They're afraid that the boss won't believe them. Don't take this personally, but if you are having these thoughts, you are probably a world-class ditz and you should get help in the form of having your brain replaced with styrofoam packing peanuts or Weed-Be-Gone. Whether or not he or she believes you is not the point. Studies have shown that even when the excuses are legitimate, bosses generally don't believe you. They do, however, tend to be easier on people who are creative. In fact, most bosses consider excuses a form of tax-deductible entertainment. This concept has been further supported by recent I.R.S. rulings that allow significant portions of flaky employees' salaries to receive additional business tax credits if it can be shown that their excuses were a form of entertainment. (IRC 1. DORK a. FLAKE)

"I like to to think of it as
the screenplay for a
smash hit in Hollywood."

2

How to Use This Book

As thousands of politicians can (and do every day) testify, there is nothing in this world more devastating than being in a tight spot with no previously rehearsed, well thought-out excuse. From Richard Nixon to Ted Kennedy, from Bob Packwood to Hillary Rodham Clinton, from Woody Allen to Jim Baker (not actually politicians), people of all walks of life stand as crumbling pillars of pathetic proof that well-delivered excuses are the very essence of a successful life. They know that if you have to pause, roll your eyes and think,...you're dead. If you can't deliver the excuse quickly, confidently, even professionally, the public perceives you as a real weenie.

If you think things are bad if you come up

with a lame excuse, try telling the truth sometime! If you should ever attempt to wade into these murky waters, you will be grappling with two insurmountable problems: First; absolutely no one will believe you, and second; everyone will consider you the office dork for not being able to come up with a more imaginative excuse.

As you can see, your only realistic choice is to be prepared on a split-second's notice with an interesting, creative, and, most important, professionally written excuse. As with developing any worthwhile skill, there is a fundamentally correct way for you to get from where you are to where you want to be without developing a bunch of bad habits. We recommend that you become familiar with the following procedure precisely as it is outlined.

Procedure

Step 1: Commit each excuse in this book to memory

These excuses are one hundred percent tried and proven by some of the premier liars in the world. You will look amateurish by comparison if you try to think up your own. In fact, some of these have been tested as many as 2 or 3 times on some pretty intelligent bosses and pets, not to mention mirrors and furniture.

Important Point

There is a very important point that needs to be made here. If you should choose to go with your own excuse instead of one of these and it should fail, who do you blame? If you were to actually get caught in this situation, you would have to assume complete personal responsibility for what happens. Nobody wants that.

If, by some quirk of fate, one of our excuses should fail, you can rant and rave, you can blame and complain and have a good tantrum, and you will be completely justified in doing it because IT'S NOT YOUR FAULT! How could you possibly put a price-tag on that kind of peace of mind?

By the way, if I should personally make a mistake, it's probably because today I was upset because a whole bunch of my hair fell out and my wife left me because she says I whine too much, and I'm having a hard time concentrating since I developed adult onset dyslexia, shingles, and gingivitis, and because I'll probably have to have a tetanus shot because my hamster bit my lip while I was feeding it its medicine.

Step 2: Practice, practice, practice

Excuse making is a highly technical skill. Just like learning to throw a 90 mile per hour fast ball or getting someone to buy an appliance that they don't need, those who become masters in the art of excuses will have paid a dear price. They will have hundreds of hours of creativity-stifling, mind-numbing, and monotonous drudgery behind them. But then, if you must sacrifice to achieve something, what could possibly be more worthwhile than becoming the super-bowl champion of excuse making?

Practice on your friends. Practice on your wife or husband. Practice on total strangers and inanimate objects. Practice until everywhere you go, people will turn and walk the other way because they know that their sense of right and wrong, their intuition, their common sense is no match for your brilliant, polished, slick excuses.

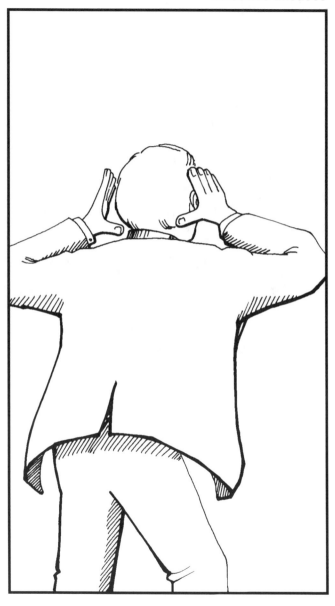

3 The Excuses

Although we have put together a work here that we believe can relieve you of the need to do any of your own thinking, and although a few of these excuses have previously been successful when used on actual people, we offer no guarantees of your individual success. You agree in-facto (impressive legal word) to use these excuses at your own risk. We accept no actual responsibility for the success or failure of any particular excuse, use only as directed. Void where prohibited by law. We are required to place this disclaimer at this critical point because we have no control over some pretty important factors in the highly technical excuse-making process. For example, we have no control over your delivery of the excuse (a key factor in its

19

success or failure), and let's be honest, there are some of you who, for the multi-million dollar salary of a talk-show host, couldn't look convincing if you put tape on your glasses, wore a pocket protector and tried to convince Arsinio Hall's audience that you are a geek. We also have no control over other things such as latent hostility in excuse receivers at the point of delivery, a superior's personal dislike for you, conniving colleagues, or stupid looks.

With these words said, the excuses, in no particular order, follow.

Excuses For Being Late

As I was leaving the men's room this morning 15 minutes before starting time, I whirled to leave and my foot slipped on some organic matter. Wouldn't you know it, my shoe got hopelessly stuck in the bottom of the urinal. I tried every way I know to get it free, but the longer it stayed in there, the more the water made the leather swell. I finally managed to work my foot out of my shoe and then the shoe came easily. I was yelling in there, didn't anyone hear me?

- - - - - - - - - - - - - - - - - - - -

As I was trying to chisel the ice trays out of the freezer, I was sticking my tongue out like I always do when I work. Wouldn't you know it, my

tongue got caught on the inside of the freezer. I
had to free myself with the hair dryer. I was able to
avoid serious injury by taking my time and not
being in too big of a hurry.

- -

I was busy throwing up broken glass outside
Mel's Tasty Freeze downtown. I have a pretty
tough stomach so I wasn't seriously injured. I've
heard that lots of people are making big bucks
suing Jack In The Box restaurants so I planted
some rat hairs, broken glass, and a bloody glove
over there to be used as evidence and then had to
take time to call a lawyer.

- -

I stopped to help a distressed motorist and it
turned out that it was a lady in the final stages of
labor. I stayed to deliver the baby and see them
safely to the hospital. It was a beautiful little girl.
Could I please go wash my hands?

- - - - - - - - - - - - - - - - - - - -

I fell in a sewer hole. It took some time to
crawl back out and then I had to run back home and
shower and change my clothes. Luckily, I wasn't
seriously hurt.

- - - - - - - - - - - - - - - - - - - -

A two hour segment of my life simply

vanished. One second it was 6:00 a. m. and I was hurrying to get ready to come to school and a split second later it was 8:00. All I can figure was that I was abducted by aliens who flew me all over the universe in a time warp and then returned me to this present dimension, or as near to it as they could. They were just off a couple of hours.

- - - - - - - - - - - - - - - - - - - -

My husband (or wife) died early this morning in my arms. I really needed a couple of extra hours to get over my grief, but now I'm OK. Just give me a good work project to take my mind off from it.

- - - - - - - - - - - - - - - - - - - -

My brother, who was shot down over Vietnam in the late 1960s was finally freed from a communist prison after over 25 years. He called from Singapore to tell us that he's all right and I just couldn't get him off the phone. You know how that can be. I dropped every hint I could think of, but he just had so much that he wanted to talk about that I couldn't be rude. They're in a way different time zone so it didn't occur to him that it was time to go to work over here.

- - - - - - - - - - - - - - - - - - - -

This morning my wife's appendix burst. There was no one there but me so I had to stay and remove it. I couldn't very well just leave her there to die. Even then I wouldn't have been so late except it took me longer to stitch her up than I thought because all I had to work with were some toe nail clippers and a spoon and I had never done it before without anesthetic. Don't worry, she seems fine now. Could I go wash my hands?

- - - - - - - - - - - - - - - - - - - -

As I was driving to work, I noticed some thieves knocking off a bank. Naturally I stopped to help. I caught the first one quickly, but it took a while for me to chase down the one in the getaway car. He had a real fast car and this time of day there is quite a bit of traffic and I didn't want to get any one else hurt so I had to be careful.

- - - - - - - - - - - - - - - - - - - -

I was on my way to work when I noticed the police and a crowd of people were trying to talk this guy out of jumping off a 15th story ledge. I stopped to offer my help and wound up going up on the ledge to talk to him. It turned out that we have the same ex-wife and a number of similar health problems, so we had lots to talk about. I tried to hurry so I wouldn't be late, but you know how people can talk sometimes. He came down with me an hour later. Sorry it took so long.

By the way, could I get off a couple of hours

early today? His analyst asked if I could come in and help with his psychotherapy. He's at a critical stage just now and he thinks that together, we can reduce the frequency of these suicide attempts.

- - - - - - - - - - - - - - - - - - - -

      This morning, just as I was walking out of the house, I got a call from a neighbor across the street. He asked me to look outside. There was what looked like a drug deal going on out on the street. I called the police and told them that I would tail the one guy until they could get there. I followed him clear across town to a warehouse. The police and I got there just in time to catch the biggest drug king-pin from Columbia. There was this really radical gun battle.

      In spite of all that, I still would have only been a half hour late, but they asked me to stay and help dis-arm a bomb that had been set under one of the policemen's cars. So that took a little longer.

- - - - - - - - - - - - - - - - - - - -

      I got a special delivery package early this morning that was addressed to Sheik Ammaal, who I didn't even know. It looked really suspicious, so I hurried down to the post office first thing. I figured I'd just have time to swing by there on my way in to work this morning and still not be late. Anyway, it turns out that it was full of weapons-grade nuclear fuel that was destined for the Middle East, so it was lucky that it had been mailed to me instead by mistake. The reason I'm late is that I had to stay and be debriefed about my relationship to the Sheik. I didn't even know the guy, but it took some talking to convince the C.I.A. guy there. Then after that, I had to take a minute and be detoxified so as not to contaminate all of you here at work. Could I go wash my hands?

- - - - - - - - - - - - - - - - - - - -

I have a habit of calling the newspaper each week to make sure that the cute little Humane society puppies that they advertise have found a home. It turns out that this week, no one claimed this little Cocker Spaniel with a sore leg. He was scheduled to be put to sleep at 8:00 this morning. I couldn't very well let that happen, so I called my cousin Bernice who said that she would give the puppy a good home. She didn't have any transportation, so I had to take her in to pick up the dog on my Vespa. Then we had to wait for half-an-hour while it got spayed. It would have taken longer, but I finally stepped in to give the vet some help. Could I please go wash my hands?

25

Excuses for Not Making a Commitment

Until I get my sociopathic, paranoid schizophrenia, Oedipus Complex, and bed wetting under control, I wouldn't feel right about dragging someone else into my messed-up life.

- - - - - - - - - - - - - - - - - - - -

As a veteran of the War On Poverty, Bud Bowl III, and 10 years of the 11:00 News, I suffer from latent battle fatigue and problems from repeated exposure to chemicals, which have rendered me physically and emotionally unable to make a long-term commitment.

- - - - - - - - - - - - - - - - - - - -

My spiritualist tells me that in my previous life, I was a squirrel. And I'm most likely coming back as a chicken.

- - - - - - - - - - - - - - - - - - - -

For all we know, tomorrow I could be walking along and an earthquake could hit and the ground could swallow me right up, or terrorists could abduct me and I could disappear without a trace. I could never live with myself if I put you through that kind of trauma.

- - - - - - - - - - - - - - - - - - - -

Scientists have proven through DNA tests that millions of years ago, humans' progenitors were sea cucumber-like creatures and trilobites. I couldn't bear the thought of someone as classy as you spending the rest of your life with someone related to an insect or worm.

Excuses for When You Lose Your Cool

I just changed my medication from Quaaludes to NoDoz.

- -

I was up all night last night negotiating the release of a group of orphans who were being held hostage. We didn't flush the terrorists out until 6:00 this morning and so, I haven't had any sleep.

- -

I'm dying from brain cancer. They cut back my pain medication because I was fading in and out of consciousness and wanted to enjoy my life as best I can. Without the medication, I suffer terribly from the intense pain, which, as you can imagine, makes me a little cranky.

- -

I bought the lottery ticket that would win $15,000,000.00 this week and I can't find it. I was up all night looking for it. You can't even imagine what a frustrating thing this is to deal with.

- - - - - - - - - - - - - - - - - - - -

During the cold war, I was captured by the Russians, who implanted a device in my brain which they communicate with by remote and which allowed them to force me to do things for them. Even though the device has been de-activated, it still causes me to have bizarre behavior and headaches sometimes.

- - - - - - - - - - - - - - - - - - - -

I was only pretending to be upset. I was experimenting to see how you would react.

- - - - - - - - - - - - - - - - - - - -

As I put my shoe on this morning, a very large scorpion crawled out without my noticing it. It crawled up my leg and stung me on the hemorrhoid. I have been so distracted over this that I lose my temper more than normal.

- - - - - - - - - - - - - - - - - - - -

After being at a Willy Nelson concert for four hours, I didn't feel well last night, and so I went to the doctor, and he discovered that my two adenoids, my thyroid gland and a bunch of lymph nodes had mysteriously exploded.

My wife fixed my favorite sweet and sour liver, anchovy and eggplant casserole last night for supper. Today, for some reason, I have some of the worst gas I've ever had and it's made me uncomfortable and out of sorts.

- -

I have been having a lot of flashbacks from the torture-murder of my cat, Skippy, a few years ago. They just keep haunting me and I haven't been getting my sleep.

Excuses for Having a Dirty House

All of the things that you see in piles are actually vitamin enriched. We are allowing them to compost so that they can be used as special plant fertilizer to grow plants that have a chemical in them that is believed to fight AIDS.

- -

We came home last night and the place looked like this. Apparently there were some Mafia types looking for some microfilm or something who really tore the place up. They finally figured out that they had the wrong house and so they left, but just look at the mess they made.

29

A tornado touched down right outside our window just for a split second. This is the only place in town that was hit. It sucked everything out of drawers, cupboards, and boxes where we had it neatly put away and piled it like you see here. At least we still have our health.

- - - - - - - - - - - - - - - - - - - -

I thought everyone had heard of this great business opportunity. People are making thousands of dollars growing fungus, worms, and mushrooms in their homes. All of this stuff you see here will soon be covered with nitrogen-enriched spores which we will sell for a small fortune. We have to see that it doesn't get disturbed though, or it will ruin the crop. Excuse me, I need to wash my hands.

- - - - - - - - - - - - - - - - - - - -

Last New Years, I made a resolution never to clean my house again until all of the children have grown up and gone. I decided it was just a waste of time to clean when they could mess it up again faster than I could clean it up. I got my inspiration from Phyllis Diller, who said "Cleaning the house while children are growing is like shoveling the walks while it's still snowing." Come back in 16 or 17 years. I'll clean it then.

30

A few days ago, we had a major flash flood come down the street and right through our house. It deposited sediment from the dairy up the street clear up to the ceiling. It has taken us days to shovel out the Bovine fecal matter and clean the walls, floor, and ceiling. If you think it smells bad now, you should have smelled it a couple of days ago. All of these items that you see scattered around my house have been drying out from the flood. In just a few more weeks, they will be dry enough to be cleaned up and then I'll put them away.

- - - - - - - - - - - - - - - - - - - -

My house? But this isn't my house. I just stopped by to see if I could sell some light bulbs.

- - - - - - - - - - - - - - - - - - - -

The reason my house looks like this is because I saw our neighbor Martha's house. It was such a mess and I didn't want her to feel bad so I came right home and messed mine up too, out of sympathy and respect for her.

- - - - - - - - - - - - - - - - - - - -

I am on strike protesting my role as the housekeeper here. No one appreciates me, so until I get some respect, I'm not ever cleaning again.

31

I have a fun hobby that you should try. I'm a pest and rodent watcher. I'm trying to see how many different varieties that I can attract so that we can photograph and catalogue them. That one over there is a very rare roach-rat cross. They are extremely difficult to breed in captivity.

- -

I'm not who you think I am. Do you think I'm (your name here)? I've had a number of people tell me how much I look like her. I've heard that her house is always so neat and clean.

Excuses for When Your Stomach Makes Noises

It must have been the live toads and snails I ate this morning.

- - - - - - - - - - - - - - - - - - - -

That noise can't possibly be my stomach. I had it removed last year to lose weight.

- - - - - - - - - - - - - - - - - - - -

Being on a tight budget, I found this great deal on garbanzo beans and brussel sprouts. I wound up buying 200 pounds of each and a cook book called "50 Interesting Ways To Prepare Beans,

Brussel Sprouts, and Rutabaga."

Excuses for Forgetting a Birthday or Anniversary

I had my friends deliver me inside a cake to your doorstep. When I jumped out, naked, I discovered that they had taken me to the wrong house. They paid me big money to keep repeating my performance over and over again. I just couldn't pass up the money.

When I finally got finished there, I gave my friends such clear directions to your house that no one could possibly get lost. And this time, when I jumped out, to my dismay, we were on the wrong block. This time, the people there called the police and I got arrested.

- - - - - - - - - - - - - - - - - - - -

I didn't forget your birthday (anniversary, or whatever). I just acted like I forgot, in order to test how you feel about me. My analyst told me to do things like this to build my self-esteem. My self-image has been poor because my grandparents who raised me used to do things like make me sleep out in the drain field and put belly-button lint on my cereal and make me eat it because I was a bed-wetter and an asthmatic who whined a lot.

33

I was at the bank during a hold up and the robber hit me over the head with the butt of his gun. When I regained consciousness, I had forgotten many of the details about my life. Dates and similar small things have been the last to return.

- - - - - - - - - - - - - - - - - - - -

I had over $2,000.00 worth of gifts mailed to you UPS last week. You mean they haven't come yet? I hope that huge diamond wasn't stolen, because I could never afford to replace it since it wasn't insured.

- - - - - - - - - - - - - - - - - - - -

My friends were going to surprise you by making a singing delivery to you of my gift. It turns out that they went to the wrong house. The starving Haitian refugees living there were very poor and they were so happy to get the clothes, exotic jewelry, and new Mercedes Benz that my friends just couldn't bear the thought of taking them back. So, as soon as I can save up the money again, I'll get you some new ones.

- - - - - - - - - - - - - - - - - - - -

I got exposed to a new strain of nasal herpes and the health authorities kept me locked up until they could test me. I tested negative, but meanwhile, thanks to the quarantine, I couldn't get out and pick up your gift.

- -

Some practical jokers changed all of my calendars for those kind that you can buy at the novelty store with the wrong dates on them. I finally figured out why I was missing so many of my appointments, and why no one besides me was going to church.

- -

I was trapped in an elevator for two days with a Razorback hog hunter named Floyd and his hound dog, Bess, two garlic salesmen, and a lawyer.

Excuses for Not Having an Assignment Finished

Last night our house ran out of toilet paper. I didn't think anything of it until I woke up this morning and found that some desperate person had used both sides of my paper.

- -

My computer went down because of a power surge. When it came back up, all that was

35

left on my disk were messages from aliens about experiments that they were performing on humans in Guatemala. I tried to print the messages, but there was some kind of lock on the printer and the aliens wouldn't allow it.

- - - - - - - - - - - - - - - - - - - -

I didn't have my briefcase chained to my wrist like I should have when I was walking from the parking lot in to work this morning. Of course they would pick this day to mug me and steal my stuff.

- - - - - - - - - - - - - - - - - - - -

Just before I faxed it, I had to fax a love letter from Delores to her secret lover, Steve. The fax machine got really hot while I was doing that one and so when I tried to send my work, it caught on fire and burned.

- - - - - - - - - - - - - - - - - - - -

A customer came in whose son had been kidnapped. We used the back of my papers to write a response to their ransom note.

- - - - - - - - - - - - - - - - - - - -

When I got up this morning, I found out that my mom had used it to line the bottom of the bird cage.

My sister and I have identical bags. She left this morning for a top secret flight on The Space Shuttle. I'm sure it must be in her bag. Right now she's somewhere over the north pole. I'll see if I can get it back in the next few days.

- - - - - - - - - - - - - - - - - - - -

My friend's hair caught on fire. I used the assignment to smother it.

- - - - - - - - - - - - - - - - - - - -

It was so good that I sent it to be copyrighted.

Excuses for Not Coming Home at Night

I was poisoned by someone. I wound up spending all night in the hospital and almost died because of the poison. While I was in the hospital, they lost my I.D. bracelet and then accidentally got me confused with a terminal cancer patient. They even removed a portion of my liver, spleen, and a few of my lymph nodes, which really hurt.

- - - - - - - - - - - - - - - - - - - -

The last thing I remember is when somebody sneaked up behind me and stuck a hypodermic needle in my backside. It must have had some drug in it that knocked me out instantly. When I woke up, I found I had been asleep under a pile of toxic waste. How long was I out? What time is it any way? Has any of my hair fallen out?

- - - - - - - - - - - - - - - - - - - -

I was with my friends and a friend of Stan's who is a billionaire philanthropist, was there. We were talking about how much fun it is to give away millions of dollars every year. The topic eventually came around to me. I spent all night weaving this yarn about needing a million dollars for a quadruple hemorrhoid transplant in order to save my life. At one point, he even got out his checkbook. Wouldn't you know it, my buddies told him that I was only kidding at 9:00 this morning. I stayed up all night for nothing.

- - - - - - - - - - - - - - - - - - - -

My flight was late. I was in an airplane circling Peoria all night.

- - - - - - - - - - - - - - - - - - - -

My taxi driver decided to try the "scenic route" routine on me and I caught him. Then he got lost and it took all night to find his way back.

39

I have a confession to make. For the past few years I have been used by the C.I.A.. to deliver messages to the underworld. I know it was dangerous, but it was my patriotic duty. I had to disappear for a while and couldn't safely surface until this morning. You can call them to verify my story if you want, but it won't do any good. It's standard procedure to deny any knowledge.

- - - - - - - - - - - - - - - - - - - -

I've been working so hard lately that I'm just worn out. I stopped at a stop light on 5th and Vine and fell fast asleep. People were even honking at me all night. I just woke up a few minutes ago and the car was out of gas, so I had to push my car to a station.

Excuses for Looking Bad

When I was little, a mean neighbor boy poured battery acid in my mouth and then made me eat a whole box of baking soda. It made my face break out into hundreds of little volcanoes, the kind your kids made in third grade. It's looking a lot better now though, don't you think?

- - - - - - - - - - - - - - - - - - - -

I agreed to try a new experimental treatment to prevent wrinkles. My dermatologist had me put guacamole dip on my face, then put my head in a microwave oven and turn it on for 8 minutes at the highest setting. It doesn't look so great now, but he promised me that my skin will be as smooth as a baby's butt in a few months. Does it look to you like it was hard on my hair?

- -

I was riding on the back of my brother's motorcycle on the way here. He hit a pot hole going 50 miles per hour. I went flying off the bike and landed head down in an open septic tank. Could I go brush my teeth?

- -

I passed a bunch of gangsters who were stealing a bag of groceries from a little old lady. I did what anyone would have done and stepped in to make them stop. I had to fight all three of them at the same time. They naturally got in a few licks before I could chase them off, in fact, one hit me right in the face with a parking meter that was probably stolen.

- -

I'm playing Albert Einstein in a play and this is my costume.

Some pranksters at work grabbed me and put me in a gunny sack. They took me to the woods a few miles from here and buried me. I had to dig myself out and then walk home.

- - - - - - - - - - - - - - - - - - - -

I had a terrible wreck with a truck that was carrying a combination of toxic and nuclear wastes. My face went through the windshield and then some plutonium got into the abrasions.

Excuses for Not Going Out With Someone

The large staph infection on my buttock is just about to burst. It can take days for all of the pus to drain out when that happens. I don't have any clothes that I want to see ruined, so I'm going to just stay home and sit on the toilet.

- - - - - - - - - - - - - - - - - - -

My son is coming down with rabies and we need to stay close and make sure he doesn't bite the dog.

- - - - - - - - - - - - - - - - - - -

We just received word that we have

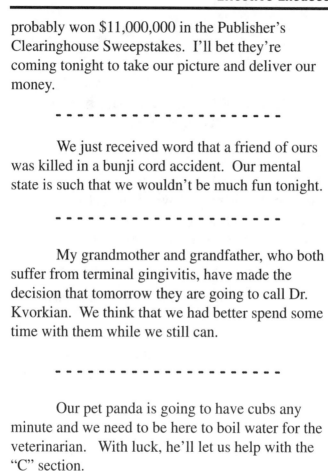

probably won $11,000,000 in the Publisher's Clearinghouse Sweepstakes. I'll bet they're coming tonight to take our picture and deliver our money.

- - - - - - - - - - - - - - - - - - - -

We just received word that a friend of ours was killed in a bunji cord accident. Our mental state is such that we wouldn't be much fun tonight.

- - - - - - - - - - - - - - - - - - - -

My grandmother and grandfather, who both suffer from terminal gingivitis, have made the decision that tomorrow they are going to call Dr. Kvorkian. We think that we had better spend some time with them while we still can.

- - - - - - - - - - - - - - - - - - - -

Our pet panda is going to have cubs any minute and we need to be here to boil water for the veterinarian. With luck, he'll let us help with the "C" section.

- - - - - - - - - - - - - - - - - - - -

I don't know whether or not you're aware that I'm actually a split personality. Lately, in the evenings, I've been becoming my dangerous serial killer alter-ego quite regularly. I'd go out, but it might not be safe.

Excuses for How Badly Your Kids Behave

We have had this terrible case of festering boils that we keep passing around the family. They just keep showing up all over their backsides. Some are just full of pus and as big as your fist. You should try to sit still with one of those!

- -

Their biological father was a stunt man.

- -

The reason they're acting like this is that my husband keeps a bottle of fleas, mosquitoes, and biting ants that he pours down their shirts whenever they don't mind him.

- -

His biological mother died at his birth from complications relating to her hyper-activity.

They are so excited because we finally let them out of the potato cellar after 5 years.

- -

I wondered about the wisdom of seasoning their food with NoDoz, horseradish, and especially those red-hot peppers.

- - - - - - - - - - - - - - - - - - - -

See that guy over there? He's an internationally known hit-man. The police are moving in on him as we speak. They asked my children to create a distraction so they could get to their positions unnoticed.

EXCUSE-O-METER™

4

How to React When You are Given an Excuse

One of the most important factors concerning your success in life is how you choose to deal with excuses when someone offers one to you. With all of the information provided here, obviously at this point, you will know all about excuses given by other people. You will understand their motivation. You will be able to clearly and professionally analyze their technique. You will probably even have committed their very excuse to memory. Now with this vast store of information at your disposal, you are prepared to make precisely the correct response to their excuse.

47

Your Possible Responses

Possible Response #1: The first possible response that you can try, should you want to, is to actually buy their excuse. This is an organizational strategy that was used from time to time before the industrial revolution, when it was widely believed that workers had some personal integrity and work ethic, but that has not seen much practical use this century. If you're into nostalgia, and, for some bizarre reason you want to look like a real sap, you might try it.

Possible Response #2: Another response that was especially popular from the mid-1860s clear into the middle of this century was to act on the philosophy that "we don't accept excuses." This approach does have some practical uses such as relieving managerial tension, because it allows a person to throw a temper tantrum, which can be therapeutic. But, again, this strategy doesn't address true 90s issues like, how will I look to everyone if I actually do throw a tantrum because everyone knows that business-related tantrums haven't been fashionable since the mid 1980s, except in the third world, and how will I feel about myself after the tantrum, and will this approach actually increase tension around the office?

Possible Response #3: (Obviously the correct

48

response): If you are a person who has the smallest degree of social skill, if you are someone who values your relationships with people in the 1990s, if you are someone who cares about the environment, world hunger, fertility rates in the third world, and our drug problem, then you will definitely want to choose response # 3 which is to simply score the excuse from 1 to 10. This is usually done by writing your score on a card and then lifting the card with the score written on it over your head with both hands so that the audience can see it.

How to Score

There are three general areas of skill that need to be taken into account when scoring an excuse. First, consider the delivery. Does the excuse maker display confidence? Did he or she get it off in a hurry without having to think? Did the deliverer stutter and stammer? Does the excuse-maker have a lot of money or anything else that you need?

Second, consider artistic expression. Was it original? Was it creative? Did it make you laugh? Is it one that you can use later on someone who hasn't heard it?

Third, was it an overall pleasing excuse? Did it serve the purpose? Did it accomplish what the excuse maker intended? Did it just "feel" good?

To be a professional excuse scorer, consider these three areas and mark your card with a black marker from 1 to 10 depending upon your evaluation.

THE BANK OF BOSNIA

...Where our tradition goes back hundreds of days to the break up of the former Soviet Union

Currently paying 240% per year on 3-day C.D.'s. Top that in your U.S. Savings Bond!

B. D. I. C. Insured. All deposits are fully insured by the full faith and credit of whichever regime happens to be in power at the moment.

Our motto: If we're still alive when you want your money, we'll make every effort to get it for you...provided the U.N. doesn't toast us first.

5 Eliminating Excuse Behaviors that will Shorten Your Life

If you will use this third strategy when you hear excuses, those excuses that you hear will never cause you the least bit of stress. You will lengthen your life expectancy by approximately your admitted weight, divided by the average number of excuses that you hear daily. If you will take it a step farther and develop your own ability to deliver good excuses as outlined in this book, if you will take this book to the cashier and pay for it instead of standing next to the book rack all day and reading it for free, you will have inched us both a centimeter closer to the vortex of life's Oz-like, Utopian self-help heaven. If you will do it right now, you will probably lose your un-wanted weight, look much better, and your kids will start treating you with respect...and the urinals at the county building might start singing "Unchained Melody." It could happen.

Summary of Excuses

If you could take all of the excuses ever made and put them end to end, then you would obviously be operating in a different dimension than people who are still living on this planet, but you would truly have something. You would have many, many excuses. These are the things that you would have. Use them. Dream of them. Use them in poetry and song, but use them. Since we are beginning to ramble, it's obvious that we have run out of things to say about excuses. At this point it's doubtful that we could even make anything up that would be very useful. So we would like to move on with a transitional quote from a wise old sage that was said at an earlier time when excuses were truly excuses, men were men, and girls were only safe in trees; if we could only remember it. But since my pet hamster caught a bladder infection which we have to drain with a straw while giving it a little hamster vinegar and Drano enema every four hours, and since the vet is charging us a thousand dollars every couple of weeks for lab tests on the urine, which, incidentally isn't as easy as you might think to get out of a rodent, and since we've been trying to get the samples and it's taken so much of our money, and caused our family a great deal of stress, you shouldn't expect us to perform at our best.

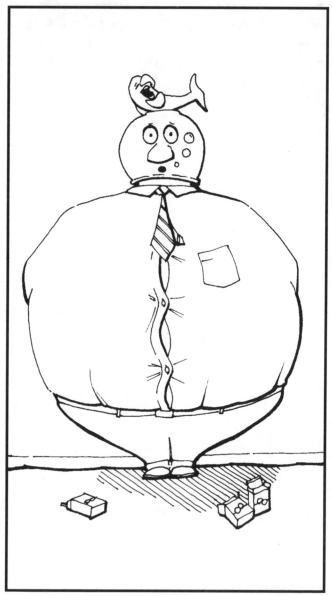

6

When Excuses Have Failed- or Tips On Successful Groveling

(Warning! This chapter has been determined to be disgusting and is not intended for readers with class, taste, friends, or an expensive European automobile.)

Groveling is the final skill that a person must to master in order to be an effective excuse maker. Good groveling becomes the skill that can save a person's reputation, career or life when, due to circumstances beyond their control, they run in to an excuse receiver who is in a bad mood, is a bank economist, college professor, or member of a grand jury, and therefore has no sense of humor, or for some other reason doesn't appreciate good excuse skills.

The Proper Mind Set

In order to grovel properly, a person must simply develop the proper mind set; they must feel like complete pond scum,...like an arm pit hair,...like soiled Odor Eaters,...lower than a good bacterial infection. In order for a normal, emotionally healthy person to develop an attitude like this, they have two options. They can either choose the hard way, allowing themselves to be strapped to a chair being forced to watch 6 months of un-interrupted day time talk shows, or they can follow the easier method, exercise a little mental discipline and do the following exercises:

First, if you are a groveler-in-training, you should find a quiet place and sit cross-legged on the floor, all the time imagining how you would feel being accused of being a lawyer. Next, picture yourself as a totally principle-free career politician who makes all of his or her decisions by polling probable voters to find out what they want to hear and then telling them. * Note: Unless you have been pronounced ethically impaired, you may find yourself becoming nauseated during this process. If you do, just take a deep breath and try to relax, allowing your mind to think of something more pleasant like having the network find a replacement for Barbara Walters or the sound of your car backing over the neighbor's cat. In a few hours, with some effort and maybe some extra medication, you will eventually get over the sensation and be able to continue training.

Now, once you stop twitching, imagine that you're on the newest Disney World ride, The Septic System of Tomorrow. (That's the one where you are tied to the end of a plumber's snake, the device that is unwound down into your toilet and through your sewer pipes in order to unclog sludge), taking a trip through the sewers. Or imagine that you're stuck inside of a plunger when it's being used, or on the end of your four-year-old son's finger.

Finally, after a few minutes of this, but before you start to feel like you want to throw up again, imagine that your wife or husband has left you because he or she thought Roseanne Barr was better looking. Or they ran away with an entomologist because they wanted more excitement in their life.

Once you have achieved the ultimate, low-groveling mind-set, stay in shape by getting an old pair of cowboy boots and taking yourself through a half-day session of licking the soles. After three or four hours of this, if you are normal, you will either want to end it all by eating eleven boxes of Alka Seltzer and chug-a-lugging a gallon of the green water left in the bottom of the fish tank for two months...or you will be prepared for some serious and successful major league groveling.

7

Explanations

Explanations and excuses have much in common. Explanations are exactly like excuses...only a little longer and often more complicated. Until you have become a master at making successful excuses, we don't recommend that you involve yourself in lengthy explanations. It will only get you into trouble. But still, because there are undoubtedly many readers who have become proficient excuse makers, and because for them they can be very useful, we have included a few samples of good explanations which you can study for ideas or memorize if you find yourself in a similar situation.

An Explanation for Why We Can't Borrow Anything From Our Neighbor

Golfing in our pasture has ruined the formerly congenial relationship that we had with our next door neighbor, Mildred, and given me a black eye. I'm going to teach you some principles about pastures so that you can avoid similar problems if you ever find yourself in a situation where you have a pasture...or a neighbor.

Pastures have many uses. I, myself have used my pasture for such varied activities as changing the oil in the truck, having a picnic, playing baseball, and even feeding livestock. But probably the most dangerous use of a pasture is to use it for golf.

One day, my son and I decided that, since we didn't the have time or the money to get in 9 holes at the local golf course, we should make a course of our own in our pasture next to the house. And why not? It's a natural. I have golfed on courses that played a lot like a pasture only with greens that were shaggier. Our pasture course has plenty of lush green grass, wide fairways, and numerous challenging obstacles and hazards. Actually, we got the idea from our neighbor, Mildred Schmunk who regularly hits a dozen or so balls out into her pasture and then spends the next half our looking for them. This is how the problem began.

One afternoon, me and my boy got our golf clubs together and went to work designing our course. We started next to the road and hit our golf balls towards a clump of sticker weeds. The hole was a cow's hoof-print that was amazingly close to the size of a regular golf hole, only with slightly different dimensions. My son, Drew, hit his ball first in the general direction of the clump. After it disappeared out of site, it was my turn. I should mention here that whenever I golf, I'm always nervous for my first shot and I usually shank it pretty bad. Naturally, that's what happened this time. I hit my first shot over on our front lawn, out of bounds, only everyone knows that there is no such a thing as out of bounds in a pasture unless you're a cow.

As my son was putting his ball into the cow's footprint, I was lining up my second shot. I should also mention that I often have a problem with my second shot. While my first swing usually takes care of the first-tee nervousness, on the second shot, I'm usually so embarrassed that I tend to keep one eye on the people who are watching me, don't keep my head down, and usually shank the ball pretty bad. Normally, my second shot is worse than my first one. That's what happened this time. My ball went zinging over into the neighbor's pasture. While I was walking over to try and find my ball, my son hollered that he was tired of waiting and was just going to play on to the next hole. (That way he would get to choose the location for hole number 2. My guess was that he would put it close to wherever he hit his ball... a chip off the old block.)

In any case, when I got over to the neighbor's pasture, Mildred was dragging her golf clubs out to take her daily whack. I tipped my hat which startled her just a bit. I guess she's not used to having people ask to play through in her pasture. I think the main thing I did wrong was to make a loud noise in the middle of her back swing with my sneeze, (Hay fever is another hazard of golf in the pasture), which caused her to jump in surprise and nearly miss the ball altogether, which would have been better than what actually happened. She shanked it almost as bad as I did my first two shots. Her ball went clear over into our field.

At this point she had the look of a woman who was truly perturbed with me but who at this point was probably not dangerous. So, trying to make up for disrupting her swing by using my best golf etiquette, I asked politely if she minded if I played my ball off from her back lawn and I said "please." She didn't say anything, but from her body language, I decided that I'd better hurry. I hate to have to rush my shot like that because whenever I hurry, I make a bad shot similar to my first and second shots. This one ricocheted off from the neighbor's new pickup where it jumped onto the back lawn and flew all the way back into our pasture...wouldn't you know it, in the same exact direction as Mildred's ball.

Since I knew we would both probably be hunting for some time, and since I know that two sets of eyes are usually better than one, I invited Mildred to our pasture, suggesting that we help each other look for our golf balls. I looked up to see my son pretending that he didn't know me, finishing hole number three, which was about all that we have room for in this particular pasture. What a shame we can't come up with a couple more holes, I thought, as Mildred and I were thrashing around in the tall grass.

With this thought on my mind, and wanting to be as helpful to Mildred as possible, especially since it was my sneeze that contributed to her shank-shot going into our pasture, I was looking intently, determined to find the lost golf balls before Mildred did. Roughly where I saw them disappear, I saw a glint of something that suddenly caught my eye. As one of our cow's tails swished back and forth, back and forth, swatting those obnoxious biting flies that we get around here this time of year, it revealed a round, white object stuck right below the tail...in a real embarrassing place...even for a cow.

As the tail swished back and forth, I was pretty sure that I could see the "Lady Titleist" insignia on it. Therefore, I knew that it couldn't be my ball, because I rarely play with a Lady Titleist. In fact, I almost always play with the ones that have red stripes on them.

Accordingly, I trotted quickly but carefully over to take a look for myself. I tried my hardest to get a look at the ball stuck in the back end of the cow, all the while talking in soothing tones to the front end and sneaking quick peeks around to the back end, so as not to startle her and make the cow madder than Mildred. Finally, having had a closer look, I knew that I had achieved a twisted degree of success confirming that it was indeed Mildred's ball. I believed that I had partially redeemed myself for startling Mildred by finding her lost ball. In my excitement , I called to Mildred, while lifting up the cow's tail so she could get a good look; "Hey, Mildred, does this look like yours?!?"

At that point, events happened so quickly that they are a blur to my memory. However, being the kind of person who is happy to give a neighbor the benefit of the doubt, we will assume that she didn't mean for her club to fly through the air and whack me in the face. Nonetheless, it did and I ended up with this black eye. Instead of coming over to see her ball, and if I was OK, she was so flustered that she stomped into the house looking like a black cloud. And ever since then, the air has been pretty tense between our two pastures. And Mildred seems to have given up pasture golf.

8 An Explanation for Personal Hygiene Problems

One thing that we modern people take for granted is our cleanliness. It is an obsession. We shower every day. We brush and floss our teeth. We wash our hands after pumping out the septic tank, and we even refuse to allow our toddlers to eat the interesting things that they find on the floors of public rest rooms.

Before you go thinking that we're so neat, remember that being clean is easy for us. We have clean facilities. But our poor pioneer ancestors weren't so fortunate. Old timers remember the days when ground was just being busted up in many new farming areas and springtime was marked by constant dust storms. They ate and breathed dirt with every meal. Those who didn't live through this, or who's parents don't make them sleep in a drain field, can't appreciate real prime quality dirt.

Many people don't realize what a new thing this cleanliness is. What information exists about personal cleanliness in our history books suggests that most adults of the 18th and early 19th centuries often went decades without a shower or a bath. They rarely, if ever washed all of their body at one time and they spent their entire lives wearing the same old dirt, sweat, and clothes. Not surprisingly, they also liked their horses and dogs better than their human friends.

The embarrassing truth is that scholars and scientists of the 1700s actually taught the public that bathing was unhealthy. I guess they figured that drawing that thick heavy brown air through their abscessed, black teeth was good exercise for their lungs and chest muscles and, of course, the stench from body odor and moose breath would have kept most forms of insects and parasites away (except for friendly ones like ticks, leeches, lice, roaches, spiders, scorpions, bedbugs and mosquitoes).

In the late 1700s, one respectable Quaker lady was encouraged to try the shower that her husband had built for her in their back yard. She later wrote in her diary about the significant event, "I bore it better than I expected, not having been wet all over at once, for 28 years past."

70

By the middle 1800s, however, the stifling, reesty winds of change were beginning to blow. These old notions about the unhealthiness of bathing were being dispelled and people knew that they should bath occasionally. The colonizer, Brigham Young, for example instructed his pioneer followers during the 1860s to bath at least weekly.

The problem for pioneers was simply finding a convenient way to do it. There was absolutely no privacy along the wagon trail unless one was short enough to crouch behind sagebrush or cactus. Toilets were not a problem because pioneers could just keep an eye out for those outhouses that OSHA required be placed every few hundred yards as they traveled along the plains. The problem with these though, was that they weren't very clean and so many women were reluctant to use them. Most figured they would rather wait until they got to Oregon. The other problem was that most of their wagons didn't have shower facilities, and it was a long way between KOA campgrounds.

I have heard many modern pioneers who are still living out west tell of doing their laundry and taking their baths in irrigation canals and ditches and of hauling water in barrels for household use. My kids still think swimming in the ditches is wonderful, but then, they are the same ones who will spend all day carving neat things out of a dried cow pie or making origami designs from worms

71

when we go fishing. They also don't mind going to church with a little jam plastered on their shirts, and they complain when you dig the compost out of their ears every year when it's time to start school again.

Thankfully, we modern people have solved most of the cleanliness problems of our ancestors. However, we now have personal hygiene problems of a different "modern" nature to deal with. We must grapple with problems like; what to do with all of those craters in our ears, noses, tongues and unmentionable body parts after the current body piercing fashion trend is over. We will wonder, "Should I sheet rock over them or should I hang something in them like a plant, the kid's coats, or my tools?" and, "How do I cross through barbed-wire fences and maintain proper coolness of fashion when the crotch of my pants is dragging on the ground?" and, "After all of my teeth fall out and my lips are surgically removed from the cancer caused by smokeless tobacco, will I still need to floss?" "Why?"

Yes, I suppose that there will always be personal hygiene problems of one kind or another. This is why I think we worry way too much about how we smell and look. Why should I care that my hair has mostly fallen out and that my gums are receding so my teeth will soon all fall out? A few years ago, people stunk so bad they kept their mouth shut, held their breath...and of course, they wore a hat. Personally, I would just like to be able to time my showers to occur when someone else isn't busy flushing a toilet, or being able to wait long enough after the girls get through in the shower that I can bath in warm water.

For now, whenever I am enjoying my routine cold shower, I take my mind off from it by pausing to think about my pioneer ancestors who smelled like Limburger cheese floating in a septic tank. And I ponder the hygiene of future generations.

"Wait right here cowboy. . ."

9 An Explanation for why Women have Better Luck than Men

I believe that I have detected a double standard in our country. If some of you have observed like I have, that women are often treated differently than men, then I need for you to back me up on this because right now I am losing the argument with my wife. She insists I'm having a testosterone attack and losing my mind.

I cite as evidence of this double standard that my wife has a reputation far and wide for being a fast and reckless driver (Of course, I will need my friends, who know about this to corroborate). If I remember correctly, as a teenager, the local PTA had an emergency telephone network set up which enabled all of the moms in the neighborhood to keep an eye on her in order to protect their children. When she would roar through the area in her 68 Volkswagen beetle, women could be seen grabbing their children and diving for safety behind bushes, trees and rocks until she was safely past.

I, on the other hand, am probably the best driver I know. I have always been careful to obey all traffic safety laws. How ironic it is that when my wife gets pulled over for speeding, 4 or 5 times a week, she never gets a ticket. Smiling male police officers kindly beg her pardon and issue her a warning for the unfortunate misunderstanding and then whistle while they stroll back to their patrol cars.

In spite of the fact that I am an impeccable driver, I still get cited for such silly things as having the lights out on my rear license plate, not having enough tread on my tires, or driving the wrong way down a one-way street.

This is blatant discrimination, but it's nothing new. I believe that men have always had a raw deal. A good historical example occurred in the town of Ruby, which was a wide-open mining town in north-eastern Washington in the 1880s.

One morning shortly before dawn, one of the town's many partyers staggered drunkenly up to the main bordello and knocked loudly. When no one came, he knocked again louder and began to holler until everyone in the place was awake.

76

Finally, when it was obvious that no one would get any sleep until this fellow was taken care of, the Madame of the house came downstairs and yanked open the door scowling at the man. After a couple of minutes of arguing with this drunk and admittedly even having to fight him off, she put a sweet look on her face and asked him in a suggestive voice to wait just a minute, that she would be right back. She came back all right, and she smiled at the guy while she pulled a pistol out from under her arm and opened fire. The drunken man collapsed onto the steps in a heap with a bullet in his heart.

I believe that sexual harassment is a very serious crime. I can't even imagine the pain and agony of having some woman repeatedly misread my attempts to look nice and be pleasant and ask me out for a date totally against my wishes. I'm sure that my suffering should be worth at least a couple of million dollars, if she can afford it, but this case of the drunk guy is different. He effectively got the death penalty for sexual harassment while he was drunk! And, what disturbs me is the double standard concerning how this Madame was dealt with.

As the town lazily woke up later that morning, the body still lay in a heap. A city official who had spent the night in the house stumbled over it on the way out, hardly pausing even a moment to study it. Just then the Ruby sheriff, (a man, of course) who was beginning to make his morning rounds, happened by and saw the corpse. Quickly sizing up the situation from experience, he shrugged his shoulders and said, "probably got what he deserved." He then sent for someone to clean up the mess and haul away the remains.

Later in the day, the sheriff was accosted by a handful of concerned citizens who demanded that he go by the establishment and investigate the shooting. Obviously, he had other more important murders to investigate because characteristically, he never got around to it.

By that time, the Madame had already boarded a stage for Spokane Falls where she would spend a few days of rest and relaxation, fully expecting that when she returned, the whole matter would be entirely forgotten.

Of course, she was right. Just like my wife's driving, nothing was ever done about this murder. Imagine if that would have been a guy. He would have been dragged behind a horse or buried in an ant hill. While we're imagining, let's imagine what would have happened if a GUY had shot a drunk LADY who was bothering him. In fact you might as well imagine a million-dollar check coming in the mail because you haven't received your share of government entitlements over the years and they want to refund your taxes to make things fair, because all of this imagining won't change the fact that we men are dealt with differently than women. And what really hurts is that most of the time it's our own faults. Yes, even we men treat women differently than we do other men.

I have pondered much upon the reasons for this discrimination. Could it happen because good women are so scarce that they can't be spared out of circulation for a 6 month jail term, let alone hanged or shot. Or could it be that men feel a desire to kiss up to women so that when they do stupid things, the score will be closer to even and the men won't get yelled at. What really scares me is the likelihood that I will find that my wife is right, that all of this discrimination that I perceive is just a product of my twisted imagination. It's your call.

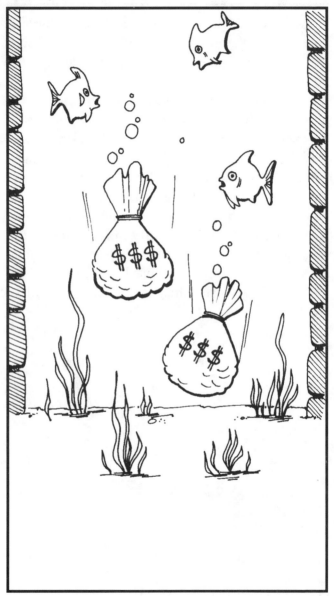

10

An Explanation for Why Everyone You Run Into Seems to be Incompetent

There is absolutely no substitute for competence. Exceptionally competent people exist in this world who can handle virtually anything. How unfortunate it is that you will never meet them, let alone have them actually do anything for you. They are only on television. The people who **YOU** are counting on, your friends and employees, the people who work on your stuff, can't get a fork into their mouth without poking it in their eye. They're the ones still trying to figure out which end of the paint gun goes in their mouth.

Don't despair. This tendency toward incompetence has been with us a long time. Even our pioneer ancestors were surrounded by idiots. In fact, I read some statistics somewhere that said that the average old west sheriff only had three working toes.

A good example is a San Diego sheriff who, despite the best of intentions, had a tough time getting things right. During the late 1800s San Diego was having a crime wave that was complicated by it's position right next to the border with Mexico. If ever they needed a competent sheriff, now was the time.

There was one robber, especially, who knew how to rob the banks and get quickly back across the border where he was safe. It looked like he would never be caught. The sheriff in San Diego at the time began to take a special, personal interest in these crimes, even to the point of obsession, and decided to set traps to catch him.

Nearly all of the robberies had happened at banks which were within a short distance of the border. Since there were only a few of these, the Sheriff had meetings with all of the staff people and arranged to have deputies within fairly close proximity at all times. They then devised an alarm system which would allow the officers to be notified quickly so that they could arrive within minutes of when a robbery was committed and catch the bandits.

Once they were thus prepared, they didn't have long to wait. Within a couple of days, one of the banks was hit by the bandit from Mexico. He cleaned them out and got on his way with over a thousand dollars in currency (quite a sum in those days). But the alarm had been sounded. Within minutes the nearby deputies were hot on his trail.

They ran their specially chosen horses hard, and during the chase even the Sheriff was able to catch up to the posse and join in. Unfortunately, although they never lost sight of the bandit, and to their dismay, they couldn't get a shot off at him before he crossed the border.

The sheriff's frustration was intense. He gave the order to follow him even into Mexico. They kept him in sight and witnessed as he disappeared into a group of shacks. The posse was so close that they could even see which one he went into. They rode right up to the shack and while the Sheriff and four deputies stood with their guns ready, a fifth pounded on the door.

Eventually, a woman came to the door and peeked out. One of the men then got his foot into the opening of the door and flung it open. The sheriff then demanded, "A man just came in here. He was witnessed robbing a bank. We want him out here right now!"

The woman simply said, "No hablo Ingles." (I don't speak English.)

The Sheriff, who had been waiting too long already to get his man, was prepared for this problem. He grabbed one of his deputies who was bilingual, to interpret. He said: "You tell the woman that we know she's hiding a fugitive and we won't leave until we have him."

To the posse's surprise, out from the back of the hut strolled a man who introduced himself as Jose, the owner of the house. The men immediately recognized him as the robber. He had a confident swagger, a sneer on his face, and said, in Spanish: "Don't worry Maria, they can't harm us here in Mexico."

This phrase the faithful deputy translated for the sheriff which made him absolutely roaring mad. He hadn't chased this guy for months and followed him across the border to have him slip through their fingers now. He leaped across the threshold and grabbed the robber around the neck, jamming the barrel of his six-shooter right into Jose's mouth. He then said to the interpreter: "You tell Jose that we followed him here from the robbery. We know he has a sack full of money here somewhere. He has 10 seconds to tell me where it is or I'll blow his head off!"

The interpreter carefully translated what the Sheriff had said. Jose, the bank robber, was now sweating profusely, terrified for his life. Everyone knew that the sheriff was upset and he meant business.

As the Sheriff counted down from 1, to 2 and then to 7, 8, and then 9, Jose blurted out in Spanish: "I threw the money in the well. Go look if you don't believe me! It's out in the well!"

With that, the interpreter turned to the

Sheriff and said coolly: "Jose says 'he's not afraid to die."

I never heard what happened next. But I suspect that, in spite of his lack of competence, the Sheriff did manage, through sheer pluck and determination, to stop the bank robberies. And we learn an important lesson: That with dogged determination, we can often overcome our bumbling incompetence...if we don't kill someone first.

11 A Lengthy, Yet Useful Explanation for Being A Poor Slob

In the latter half of the 1800s, a small group of Chinese men worked menial jobs and literally wasted their lives, running back and forth to the Columbia River in Washington State. They knew that if the water level ever got low enough that they could work the sand bars, great amounts of gold could be taken in a very short time. Only once, for just a few days, was their patience ever rewarded. And in that brief time they were able to produce enough gold dust to support themselves for decades as they literally waited out their lives for the river level to drop again. Don't be disgusted. Don't have a cow. These men, were only living their idea of the American dream.

For most people, a big part of the American

87

dream is to become filthy stinking rich. We Americans see as a part of our birthright, the privilege of starting off economically where our parents left off...and then having them support us until we are rich enough to rub their noses in it. The problem is that with fifty or sixty billion dollars leaving our country each month through trade imbalance and inflation, and with the number of people who can qualify for social security skyrocketing out of sight, it's becoming increasingly more difficult for parents to support their adult kids at a level to which they have become accustomed, at the same time they're supporting needy groups in other countries in the world until THEY get rich enough to rub our noses in it.

Some from among the ranks of the paranoid and uninitiated might perceive this as a problem. That's just because they haven't learned the secrets of how to hit it rich in America in the 1990s. Just like always, if you are a go getter who really wants to get ahead, and who is willing to commit to long hours and take big risks, you can still have the opportunity of being the defendant in frivolous civil law suits and of paying exorbitant taxes in order to support those who have a slightly different version of the American dream.

For example, one career path that has proven to really rake in the big bucks, consists of drawing a disability check for a person's first job, and moonlighting as a social security recipient for a second. One of the unfortunate realities of our time is that often, both spouses must both work two jobs like this in order to pay child support. Otherwise the income from their second job wouldn't be enough to supplement the child support payments of the former spouse of the person that they are living with. Does this sound complicated? Hey now, don't let a few trivial complications like complication discourage you from your quest to be rich enough to enable your kids to become over-indulged derelicts and burdens to society.

Yes, yes, of course I realize that for many reasons, you may be unable to work two jobs like this. Maybe you got started early in life as a small business person so that now, you are the only tax payer remaining in your precinct. You owe so much in back taxes that you can't sell your business for enough to pay them and so you're stuck. Or maybe, due to old fashioned hang-ups about responsibility or outdated feelings of love and commitment, you can't bring yourself to place the economic security of truly needy poor in jeopardy by fraudulently overburdening the welfare system. Or, it's even conceivable that your mis-guided sense of values makes you uncomfortable giving your kids everything they want without any effort on their part.

If one or more of these descriptions hits home, you should probably check with the department of social services for the name of a psychiatrist who accepts two-party entitlement checks and get yourself some help so that you can pursue the American dream while you still have a realistic chance of success.

Draining big bucks out of the government isn't the only way to become filthy rich now days either. One of these next ideas is sure to work for you. Out of a population of around 250 million a high percentage (2 or 3) have made their millions the surest way possible, by winning the lottery. In fact, right now you should probably take your entire welfare check this down to the nearest 7-11 store and buy all of the lotto tickets they have. A million or so should do it. If you can't afford to buy that many, an alternative is to buy one and just take it down to the print shop and have it copied. Or, you can buy one ticket and make a deal with a million or so of your friends that all will share in the winner's profits. Then sit back and watch Geraldo while waiting for the door bell to ring and for the lottery officials to take your picture holding your over-sized check for $50 million,...After which they will take back that phony prop check and give you the real one, your first installment of $1.00 which will come to you each and every year for the next 50 million years, which is how most lottery pay-outs work. Hey, nobody said that being a millionaire was easy.

What's that? You say that black jack dealers argue over who gets to have you at their table, that the only thing you ever gambled for and won was the time at the Sheriff's posse auction, you bought a ticket and won a free bunji chord jump off the rim of The Grand Canyon? Not to worry, we still have plenty of avenues to explore to help even bumbling idiots like yourself get rich. For example, have you considered being born that way?...On the other hand, maybe that won't work for you either since for you to succeed at this method, you would already be rich, and thus wouldn't need me to tell you how. And if you are poor, you are probably having trouble getting your parents to cooperate.

Another "trendy", although slightly bumpy road to riches is to get yourself hit by a rich person driving her Rolls Royce or Mercedes or selling your excess body parts and blood. These methods can work, but there are side effects. It does take quite a few body parts to get you filthy stinking rich. And then it can be more difficult to enjoy your hard earned millions without a heart, lungs, lenses, kidneys, and especially without your liver.

If you happen to be one of those who is squeamish about trying these modern fund raising methods, maybe it's time that you stopped counting

91

on that risky modern stuff and come full circle. Apply the get-rich-quick scheme that we started this article with and that your pioneer ancestors used successfully time and time again: Namely, go off on a gold rush.

Now hold on just a minute. Put away all visions of 16 hour days slaving away down in the bowels of the earth under creaking timbers on the wrong end of a pick. This strategy doesn't need to be that tough. The last thing you need is a real gold mine. All you need is a good rumor. In fact, I know right now of a number of great places you could go to begin your search. For instance, a group of successful miners buried some gold near Quincy, Washington that's never been found.

Just find a nice isolated spot, salt a little gold around, yell "Gold!" as loud as you can. Then sit back and make your fortune the safe way, by selling supplies, booze, mining equipment and pretty girls to the miners at triple their fair market value. Incidentally, this method also works with skiing, firefighters, UFO sightings, and places where historic figures like Washington, Lincoln, Kennedy and Frank Zappa have slept, eaten, or camped...and with penny stocks.

Consider carefully. If you are one who has been missing out on the financial portion of your American dream, now is the time to start. You can either grab your back-hoes and other earth moving equipment, and start immediately digging randomly and frantically around the town of Quincy. Or you can choose a more 90's type method. This is your chance.

"Class. . . you're falling behind"

12 An Explanation for Why School Teachers Should be Responsible for Delinquent Kids

It's a good thing that we teachers aren't prone to whining and complaining because the profession has major challenges. Impossible expectations, low compensation, poor color coordination, delirium tremens, bleeding ulcers, and having to spend the summers goofing off all add to teachers' traumas.

Teaching has always been tough. Not long ago I discovered a list of instructions for teachers of the Mason Street School in San Diego, California, from the 1887-88 school year. As you read through these, think how wonderful it is that teachers knew just what to do to earn the big bucks in the good old days.

1) Teachers will fill lamps, clean chimneys and trim

95

wicks each day.

2) Each teacher will bring a scuttle of coal and a bucket of water for the day's use.

3) Make your pens carefully. You may whittle nibs (?) for the individual tastes of children.

4) Men teachers may take one evening each week for courting purposes or two evenings a week if they go to church regularly.

5) After ten hours in the school, the teacher should spend the remaining time reading the Bible and other good books.

6) Women teachers who marry or engage in other unseemly conduct will be dismissed.

7) Every teacher who smokes, uses liquor in any form, frequents pool or public halls, or gets shaved in a barber shop will give good reasons to suspect his worth, intentions, integrity and honesty.

8) The teacher who performs his labors faithfully without fault for five years will be given an increase of 25 cents a week in his pay-providing the Board of Education approves.

Some readers may assume that today's teachers would have a hard time measuring up to these Victorian expectations and strict rules. But I believe that this is absolutely not the case. In fact, the opposite is closer to the truth. I maintain that one of the biggest problems in education today is that the cultural revolution of the 60s and 70s removed clear behavioral guidelines for teachers and students.

96

It is a fact that most teachers, like most children, even though they will sometimes deny it, crave well-defined limits and guidelines. We want to at least know who to shoot and where to spray paint. What we need more than anything else in this country (aside from a decent show on TV and something we can eat that won't kill us) is a widely accepted set of rules from our society, like those from 1887.

The truth is, we already have them. They are just not written down. While teaching, I have observed the following unwritten "de facto" rules: (School districts of America, write these down!)

1) Teachers must dress conservatively at all times. What they're wearing cannot be extreme. Since it takes time to be sure, they must always wear clothes that are at least 10 years old.

2) Teachers are to cheerfully accept all blame for the problems of society. (Teachers must be the problem because parents are so overwhelmed working two jobs while living in different states, finding themselves, hang gliding, seeking fulfillment, skiing, dealing with their mid-life crisis, and golfing that their influence on their children is negligible.)

3) If there is ever a personality conflict, argument or disagreement, or if a student doesn't want to work, the teacher is a jerk.

4) Make your classes carefully. You must prepare lessons for each student's individual taste, and

97

preferred learning style. This will certainly prepare them for a high-paying career playing video games, collecting sports cards, or hanging out with their friends. Teach them to sue whenever things aren't the way they want.

5) Since our main desired outcome, indeed our all consuming passion, is to keep students in school as long as possible, regardless of academic progress or their effect on the rest of the class, the entertainment value of classes must be spellbinding. Cable television is to be the standard against which your classes will be measured. In order to avoid constant disruption, you must be at least as entertaining as Stephen Spielberg.

6) Any teacher who publicly displays respect for the flag, our fundamental political institutions, the office of President, veterans who died for our country, or who attends church regularly, denies belief in the Great Pumpkin or admits to belief in God is definitely a bigoted, subversive, person and will give good reason to suspect his intentions.

7) Any teacher who recklessly flunks a student places himself and his entire class in danger of having the student return and shoot up the classroom with an Uzi machine gun.

8) The teacher who performs his labors faithfully without fault for five years will be given an allusion to a commitment to a promise of a possible future increase of 25 cents a week in his pay-providing the board of directors, the public, the legislature, the

governor, the committee for sound government, Uncle Harvey, the UN security council, Howdy Doody, All Caucasians on the island of Madagascar, the Pope, and the Avon Lady approve it and provided that the legislature doesn't decide that they need the money for something else first.

There they are folks, nine rules which I believe would work today in America. We must get these accepted soon, because that's the only way that our nation can ever hope to maintain its lead position as supplier of 68% of the world's fast-food work force...and if we're not careful, we could lose our majority share of the world's consumer debt.

13

An Explanation on why I Grow A Mustache

Why I have chosen to grow this mustache is a question that no one has had the courage to ask me...but I know they are all wondering about it. I can feel their little beady eyes looking at me. The problem is that it has taken me many years to understand myself, let alone comprehend well enough that I can explain to others.

In the first place, it should be noted that I don't grow a very good mustache, at least, not like some of those guys who have llama or gorilla genes and who have hair everywhere. And I don't think it's due to a lack of testosterone either. After all, I watch football, boxing, the Miss America Pageant, I fix fences, and I have loads of male-type hair growing out of my ears and nose. No, it's a

101

tolerable mustache, just nothing spectacular.

I should also mention that it itches and gets things caught in it...and my wife doesn't like it. It's a little bit of a hassle...but yet, I grow it. There are of course complex reasons why I do. And I'm sure that something like a man's desire to grow a mustache can't be explained by one simple experience or by reason alone. It's much more complicated than that. Since with me there are lots of little peripheral reasons that have contributed to the decision, let's get some of those out of the way and then we can analyze the really meaty ones.

One little reason why I grow a mustache is because facial hair isn't cool with teenagers, the ones who sag their pants and shave the sides of their heads up to beyond where most guys my age don't have any. It's my way of doing a sort of reverse adult rebellion "in your face" to them.

Another small reason is because if I stand in front of the bathroom mirror and if I can get the light to shine on it just right, I can imagine myself looking rugged and manly...especially in a good 10 gallon hat.

While the above reasons contribute to my desire to grow hair on my lip, we really haven't explored the granddaddy of all my reasons, the one that really motivates me. To understand this one, I have to take you back in time. In fact, you have to go back 20 or so years to get to the bottom line, the real reason; a tennis game.

I have to admit here that I honestly hadn't played a whole lot of tennis before. I kind of figured it was a sport for wimps. But my new bride liked to play and she kept after me until finally I relented. We were newly weds, and at least to me it was still important to make a good impression. At times I felt like I was competing with all of those guys she could have married. So when she was just about to the point of calling me a coward and questioning my manhood, I had to give in, humor her, and go play a little tennis.

We wandered over to the tennis courts, went inside, got our racquets out of their cases, and began to hit the ball back and forth...easy...just to limber up. This wasn't too bad. I discovered that I could hit it a lot harder than she could, which reassured me that I didn't need to worry about beating her. And yet, there was a nagging doubt somewhere in the back of my mind that I'm sure was influenced by this strange look of confidence combined with blood lust that was beginning to appear on her face, and which was unsettling.

The pace of the hitting gradually began to pick up as we both warmed up and gained confidence. So, in spite of the fact that this was my frail, petit, feminine young bride over there, I eventually began to really let loose and smash the ball over almost as hard as I could. Every time I wound up and smashed the ball over to her, she would authoritatively hit it back to me and ask me kindly not to hit it so hard. I naturally assumed that she was afraid or that she didn't think she could hit it back...and besides, this was kind of fun, so I ignored her. I would hit it back to her...hard, since I was a manly man and manly men show their manhood by hitting hard...and she would hit it back in a condescending sort of way, and then scold me...and then I would smash it back...and it would be returned softly...and this would go on until I made a foolish man sort of mistake and hit the ball hard...into the net or over the fence. She had long since stopped asking me not to hit it so hard. She never made those "hit it as hard as you can" kinds of mistakes. She just methodically, patiently hit the ball back right to me, without velocity, without spin, just back there, right in front of me...and I would hit it back to her hard and then she would hit it back until finally I made another mistake and hit the ball over the back stop. It was like hitting against a wall except this wall was patronizing and offered tips on my game.

As the real match began and as I was falling further and further behind in the score...I began to hallucinate. I started imagining in my mind my sweet bride saying with each stroke " remember, I told you that you should stop and ask for directions. If you had built those bookshelves the way I told you to, the way my father did, they wouldn't have collapsed," and "rinse the dishes of before you put them into the dishwasher and you won't have to wash them again by hand."

I was faced with the truth: my wife does not really need me. Just like one of the kids, she must spend the rest of her days trying to raise me, to impress on my mind all of these things that women instinctively know, that are obvious to them without even thinking things over...and that they really don't need us men for anything. Getting beaten by my delicate wife in tennis because she methodically hit every ball back to me until I made a stupid male-type of mistake was a tough lesson for me to learn. Figuring out that I am nothing more than one of the larger kids only with a paunch and a back problem was also a bitter pill to swallow. While I know that it's the truth, I still don't like it.

So this mustache is symbolic. It's a form of protest against the way things are, against a fundamental fact of humanity that I can't change. We men need women in the worst way, but they don't really need us. They only keep us around because they worry that something bad will happen to us if we're left alone. When you get right down to it, there are only two things that women can't do much better than men can: The first one is way way way beyond the scope of this article, and even now, as we speak, we are teetering on the brink of losing even this one, thanks to the rapid advances of modern medicine and science. The second one, for the time being is secure. Growing facial hair is the domain of men period. Women never intentionally compete with men in the facial hair growing department...I don't think. (Although I must confess that occasionally I meet up with one who probably could give many of us guys a run for our money if they wanted to.) But for some reason, they don't want to. That's the point.

I grow this mustache mainly as a reminder to my wife in particular, and to all the women out there in general that there is still only one thing that I can do better than they can, even if it takes no brains, planning or any useful skills, even if they don't like the way my mustache looks and it serves no worthwhile purpose, It's still something. And that makes it important to me.

Order these additional books
by Wayne Allred

- How to Cope When You are Surrounded by Idiots. . .or if You are One

-The Disgusted Driver's Handbook: Instructions for Surviving on Roads
Infested with Idiots

- Geezerhood: What to expect from life now that you're as old as dirt

 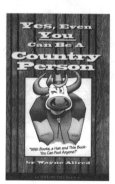 

- The Outhouse Book: Readin' that's probably not ready for indoor plumbing

- Yes, Even You Can Be A Country Person

-Whenever Your Attitude Stinks. . . Read This

- A Complete Guide to Effective Excuses

Willow Tree Book Order Form

Book Title	Quantity	x	Cost / Book	=	Total
			$5.95		
			$5.95		
			$5.95		
			$5.95		
			$5.95		
			$5.95		
			$5.95		

Do not send Cash. Mail check or money order to:

**Willow Tree Books   P.O. Box 516
Kamas, Utah   84036**
Telephone 435-783-6679
Allow 3 weeks for delivery.

Quantity discounts available. Call us for more information.
9 a.m. - 5 p.m. MST

Sub Total =	
Shipping =	$2.00
Tax 8.5% =	
Total Amount Enclosed =	

Shipping Address

Name:

Street:

City: State:

Zip Code:

Telephone: